BOOK
MARKETING
BASICS

10 Simple Marketing Tips That Work

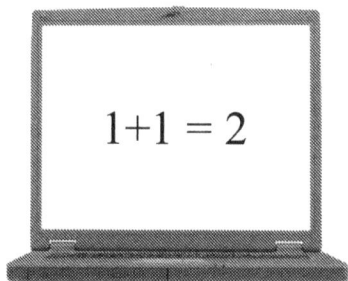

$$1+1 = 2$$

*The New Model for Promoting
Your Book*

Rodney Charles

Book Marketing Basics

The New Model For Promoting Your Book

Rodney Charles

© Rodney Charles 2007

Published by 1stWorld Publishing
1100 North 4th St. Suite 131, Fairfield, Iowa 52556
tel: 641-209-5000 • fax: 641-209-3001
web: www.1stworldpublishing.com

First Edition

LCCN: 2007931427
SoftCover ISBN: 978-1-4218-9996-1
HardCover ISBN: 978-1-4218-9997-8
eBook ISBN: 978-1-4218-9998-5

With Appreciation for:

My co-adventurers Nandini, Anya, Aman and sleepy Squirtle

What I have learned and taught about writing, publishing, distribution and marketing has been influenced by two undisputed mentors in the Publishing Industry: Dan Poynter and John Kremer. For anyone planning a career in writing or publishing, it is essential to digest the volumes of material these two pioneers have collected and organized.

This simple book was written to:

INSPIRE

EDUCATE

ASSIST

anyone who has dreamed of success.

"Next to doing the right thing, the most important thing is to let people know you are doing the right thing."

—*John D. Rockefeller*

L I S T E N

"Understand that you need to sell you and your ideas in order to advance your career, gain more respect, and increase your success, influence and income."

—*Jay Abraham*

CONTENTS

3 Essentials

There are 3 things that you need to succeed as a published author. And by succeed I mean earn enough money through book sales to allow you to continue writing full time.

1. NETWORKING: You need FRIENDS. You need Friends to tell their friends to tell their friends ...about your book.

2. NETWORKING: You need to be inspired. Inspired people attract people.

3. NETWORKING: You must tell everyone. You must tell them, tell them again and keep telling them every day.

> "Selling your books is essentially a matter of making friends, lots of friends"
>
> **—John Kremer**
> Book Marketing Update

If you possess INSPIRATION and a NETWORKING PLAN, you are sure to succeed.

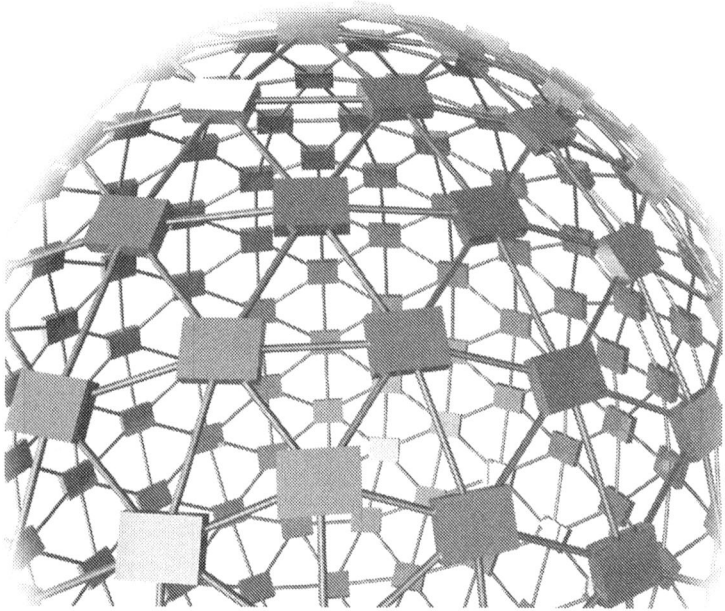

PART 1

NETWORKING

IT'S ALL ABOUT NETWORKING

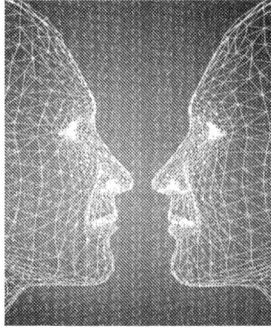

Networking is simple. It's simple because it's fun. By the time most authors have completed their books and labored through the publication process, they are so excited it is impossible to stop them from talking about what they have written ...and that is as it should be. Ultimately networking is nothing other than talking about your book.

> If you want your books to sell, and to keep on selling, then talk about them and keep on talking about them. The moment you stop talking, your books stop selling.

So you say you are too busy to network. Well, welcome to the club. So is every author who has ever succeeded with his or her book. But you are lucky. The times have changed, and it is now possible for you to succeed for 2 important reasons:

1. The New Model for promoting your book is all about the miracle of email and the Internet.

2. Networking only takes a few minutes every day

Don't let anyone convince or confuse you. It is not that hard and you CAN do it.

Let me digress for a moment. When I started my career as an author, I knew nothing about marketing and less about networking. My marketing plan consisted of traveling to as many cities as I could possibly afford and doing as many book signings as I could set up. This was the nature of marketing back before the internet made everyone on the planet our neighbor.

After 16 years of experience in the publishing world, this simple plan still remains the most effective. It is the one singular plan used by every successful publishing company in this industry: THE BOOK TOUR.

Touring is the tried and true method for selling books, because ultimately, IT IS ALL ABOUT NETWORKING. But our lives are so much busier than they have ever been and very few people have the luxury of time and the ability to travel from city to city; hence, The New Model for Promoting Your Book. Done properly, it can be every bit as effective as a book tour and sometimes more so.

> The book industry is basically a very grass-roots industry. Word of mouth is responsible for 70% of all books sold.

The book industry is basically a very grassroots industry. Word of mouth is responsible for 70% of all books sold. Most of the books that you have purchased in your lifetime were probably recommended to you by someone, either a friend, or over the radio, TV, or in school. In the past, the book tour allowed authors to start the grassfires of marketing. When an author appeared in a bookstore, he or she met people who were interested in similar subject matter and genres. The bookstore personnel and the managers all listened to the author's presentation or reading, and if they liked what they saw they made a point of keeping their shelves stocked with that author's books. Likewise, when the audience liked what they saw and heard at a book signing, they would talk to the author and invite them to reading groups, church gatherings, classrooms, workshops, symposia, radio stations, TV shows, newspaper/magazine offices...and that is classical networking.

Today all the old rules have changed (it would take another book to explain the changes and innovations in the book industry), but the basics are the same. Authors just need to keep the process of networking alive and vital if they want to continue selling books.

> Authors just need to keep the process of networking alive and vital if they want to continue selling books.

Today there is a New Model for Promoting Your Book. There are thousands of ways to network and market a book without having to empty your savings account. All you have to do is let your creativity and enthusiasm take the lead role. If you take just a few minutes every day to follow the 10 simple, tried and true recommendations that follow, your success will be directly proportional to your enthusiasm.

If your enthusiasm is off the charts,
your sales will be off the charts

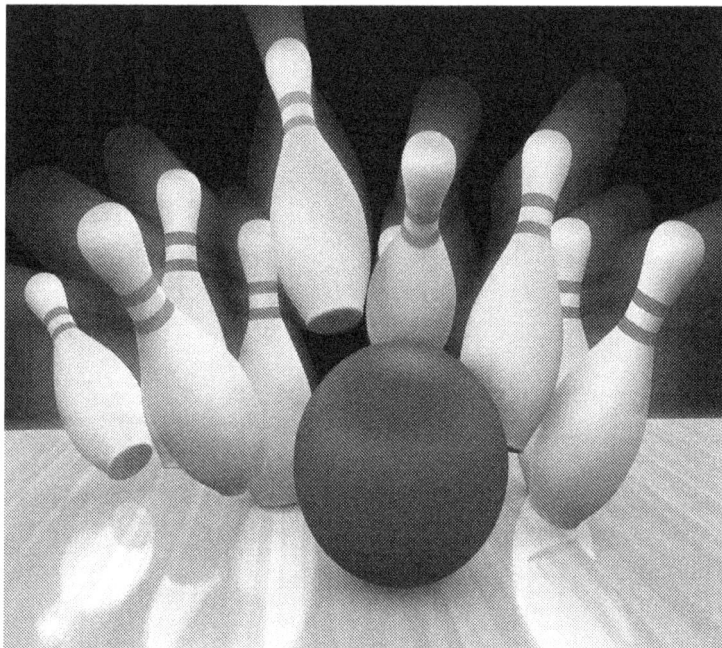

10 Simple Marketing Tips That Work

PART 2

THE NEW MODEL
FOR PROMOTING
YOUR BOOK

1. EMAIL SIGNATURE

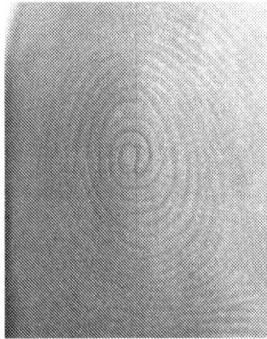

Now that your book is ready to be sold, everyone you know should be informed. One of the simplest, most effective, non-intrusive ways to sell your book is to add your web page link to the signature section of your email program. It is simple to set up, doesn't cost a dime and it automatically sends out a message to everyone you would normally email on a daily basis, so there is really no extra work involved. You'll be delightfully surprised by how many will people call or email a reply with questions about your book. This simple method frequently leads to excellent networking opportunities, and it is quite common to be contacted to speak at an event, on the radio, or even to have a book signing arranged because a friend of a friend of a friend forwarded your email to someone on his or her list.

It is important not to be shy about your book. If no one gets informed that your book exists, how would anyone know to purchase it? I repeat: the book industry is a very grassroots, word-of-mouth industry. Most of the books you have purchased in your life were probably recommended to you by a friend or by fellow readers. What you have written about will find its way to those people who are interested because you have taken a few simple steps to start the word of mouth process. Typically, your email signature should look something like the signature below:

John Smith
Author of *Life with Monkeys*
Purchase my book at: **www.1stworldpublishing/bookstore/johnsmith**
Phone: 123-456-7899
Fax: 123-456-7899

2. EMAIL CAMPAIGN

A slightly more advanced version of the simple email campaign involves adding graphics for color and design appeal and/or special offers that would entice the reader to buy your book. For example, your email could have a picture of the front cover of your book and a brief introduction to it. You can also offer free ebook copies of your book or perhaps a free consultation with the author (you!). Do whatever works comfortably for you.

> Do Not Hire Spammers.

One of the most successful techniques ever used in marketing is... to tell the truth. Simply tell people you are promoting your book and ask them to forward your email to everyone on their email list and so on.

Believe it or not, this works VERY well. Likewise, asking everyone you meet, via email or otherwise, to buy as many copies as they comfortably can works like a miracle. People love to help other people. Frequently, they just don't know how. Telling them helps them to help you.

> People love to help other people. Frequently, they just don't know how. Telling them helps them to help you.

Below is a simple example of an effective email ad campaign:

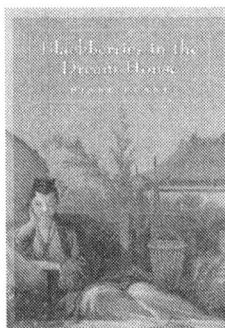

"What would happen to us if we were to undertake the discipline of turning our life entirely and self-consciously into a poem? Through Yukiko, who becomes both a contemplative Buddhist and a geisha skilled in the refinements of sensuous pleasure, Diane Frank allows us to live within the soul of a young woman who has undertaken to create a life imagined and expressed as a poem, in every moment, waking and sleeping, making love or meditating. With its power of language, Blackberries in the Dream House will seduce many readers into considering whether a prosaic life is the only choice we have."
—Pierre De Lattre, author of *Walking on Air* and *Tales of a Dalai Lama.*

"Diane Frank's exquisite sensibility manifests throughout in Blackberries in the Dream House; it is both erotic and metaphysical. In fact, her great strength is that for her there's no division between the two. The result is this fine lyrical novel."
—Stephen Dunn, Pulitzer Prize-winning poet

ISBN: 1887472681
Pages: 184
Editions: Softcover: $17.95

Buy it at: http://www.1stworldpublishing.com/store/product.aspx?ukey=0897b84c-dd20-457e-9449-7d7f8842e667

3. ONLINE REVIEWS

Another simple and effective way to draw more attention to your book is to make sure you are represented on at least the two major online booksellers: Amazon **http://www.amazon.com** and Barnes and Noble **http://www.barnesandnoble.com.** We will make sure your book is registered with these retailers, but you should go to these sites, find your book page, and add your comments in the section that allows you to review your own book. You should also ask every friend, family member and stranger (anyone who is familiar with your book) to visit the same web pages and review your book online. The more reviews you get, the more impressive and enticing your book will appear to prospective buyers. This is an effective way to draw attention to your book, and it costs absolutely nothing.

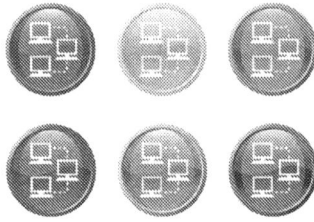

> The more reviews you get, the more impressive and enticing your book will appear to prospective buyers.

Both Amazon.com and BarnesandNoble.com have an "email this book cover to a friend" button on every book product page. This feature allows you to send anyone an email of your book cover along with an announcement that the book is available for purchase on a major website. The email will be sent to any email address that you provide and appears as a professional Book Announcement sent from Amazon or Barnes and Noble.

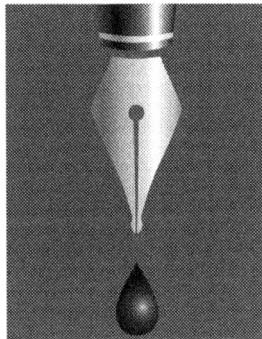

4. CREATE YOUR OWN WEBSITE

Using 1stWorld Publishing's New Model for Publishing, you are no longer printing a large quantity of books, enduring the shipping and handling costs, and then handing them over to fee-based distributors on a consignment basis (see **www.1stworldpublishing.com**).

Likewise, you no longer need to promote your book the traditional way: sending out expensive press packets, flyers and at least 500 review copies of your book to the elite media members of Don't-Call-Us-We'll-Call-You.

Today's authors build a website and use broadcast email to invite reviewers and potential buyers to come to their sites to see, try or buy books or services. Promoting electronically saves you the expense of printing and postage fees and is significantly faster. You will often receive responses, sales or inquiries the same day.

Keep your website simple, but include the necessary information to help your potential customer make a buying decision. Include:

1. An image of the front book cover.

2. An annotation for the book.

3. Special features of the book or additional services or products.

4. An author photo.

5. Author bio.

6. Contact information.

7. Most Important: a link to buy the book.

> It is better to have a link on your site that allows customers to purchase the book elsewhere, otherwise you will be overwhelmed with processing credit cards, shipping, billing, inventory, damage returns, doing customer service, etc. Let us help you sell your books: **www.1stworld-publishing.com/bookstore**

Surf the Web: Find sites that relate to your own work. When you find a match, contact the owner and recommend an exchange of links. It's all about networking.

Participate in newsgroups: Get involved and meet people who share your interests and pursuits. Cut and paste your relevant content right from your book. For a list of newsgroups, see **http://www.excite.com** and **http://www.deja.com.**

Book writing, publishing, selling and promoting has changed for the better.

Now, authors, publishers and readers come out on top.

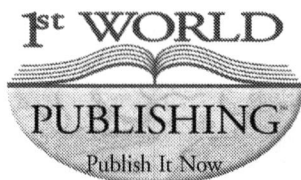

1st WORLD
PUBLISHING
Publish It Now

5. PUBLIC RELATIONS

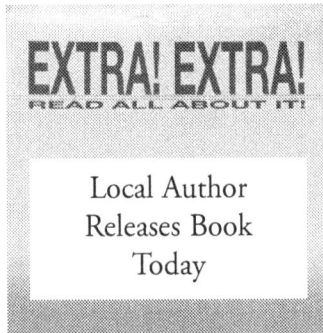

EXTRA! EXTRA!
READ ALL ABOUT IT!

Local Author
Releases Book
Today

 An effective strategy to start marketing your book is to start local. Because you are a local author, your local radio, TV and print media are far more likely to do an author interview, a book review, or perhaps a full-length article about your publication. It is vital that you saturate your local area first before moving on to a larger state-wide or national level. You need to generate favorable reviews, etc. so you can develop a Press Packet (or a digital Press Packet, which is essentially your website) for state or national media.

Spend some time and write a provocative press release (see **www.1stworldpublishing/prsamples** for sample press releases) and send it to every media outlet in your area. Normally, you can get the names and addresses of such outlets from your local Chamber of Commerce or local library, and of course, it is easily available online. **www.Google.com** and **www.Ask.com** are the best search engines to use for this. Search using the terms "Radio Stations Directory" or "TV Stations Directory" and the name of your city.

Try to tie your press release in with current news, if possible. Local media are always looking for great stories and are often required to have a certain quota of local news in their format. Getting your book reviewed, or participating in author interviews is normally quite easy for a local author. It takes very little time and is a process you can repeat over and over again. A single favorable article or radio or TV interview can lead to sales in the hundreds or thousands of copies. You just need to START the process. It has a way of snowballing on its own.

> A single favorable article or radio or TV interview can lead to sales in the hundreds or thousands of copies.

6. BOOK SIGNINGS

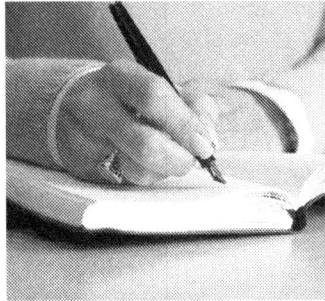

Book signings are a great way to make sure that the local media have something concrete to report about. For local authors, book signings are very easy to set up. Just call your local bookstores and tell them who you are and that you have just released your new book and are promoting it locally. They may want to take a look at the book first, so either send them to the web page we have created for you, go visit them in person, or both. Let them know that your book is available through all major distribution channels. It doesn't hurt to drop the name INGRAM BOOKS, the largest distributor of books in the world. This is where bookstores acquire 85% of all their books.

The bookstore manager is usually the person who sets up book signings. Bookstores like to do book a signing because it brings traffic to their store. So don't be shy to tell them that you are planning to contact the local media and inform them that you are doing a book signing at their store. Also, market yourself. The store manager wants to hear that you are associated with local clubs, groups, churches, or that you have dozens of family members who are planning to attend the signing. If the signing goes well, you may have sold enough copies of your book to make it onto the local bestseller lists. Naturally, that becomes the cornerstone of your future press packet or portfolio. One very important point about book signings: make sure they are interesting and successful. Don't just show up for your signing, read a few passages from your book, and expect people to buy it. Instead, add some passion to it. When you read, read it like today is your last day on earth. Many authors bring an instrument or someone with an instrument to accompany them in the background while they read. Some authors dress in period costumes (keep it dignified), bring props or slide shows or hand out bookmarkers, postcards, whistles, or anything that draws attention to the books they have published. The goal is to create an event and enjoy the book signing as much as possible. The more you enjoy it, the more the audience will enjoy it. And always remember to inform the audience that you are promoting your book and you would appreciate it if they could buy as many copies as they comfortably can. This may sound like shameless marketing, but you will receive more compliments than criticisms. You may as

well get used to the injustices of celebrity life.

> The goal is to create an event and enjoy the book signing as much as possible. The more you enjoy it, the more the audience will enjoy it.

7. FREE COMMUNITY NEWS LISTINGS

Most newspapers publish events calendars. Many of them have several calendars for different categories: business, sports, art, dining, books, current events, senior citizens, etc. Make sure that you announce the release of your book to the calendar editors. Let them know that you will be hosted on a talk show, reading at the library, or reading at a book signing. Ensure that everything that happens to you and your book gets listed in the community calendars.

Just send a short news release to the calendar editor. Keep it simple and direct. A short paragraph with the name of the event, time, date, place and a brief description are all that are needed. Don't overdo it.

Make sure that everything that happens to you and your book gets listed in the community calendars.

Wherever you may go, you can always get listed in the Calendar of Events section of local newspapers and magazines. Often, the events editor will ask you to contact another editor at the newspaper/magazine because your story ties in with an article or report that he or she might be interested in.

8. PRINTED MATTER

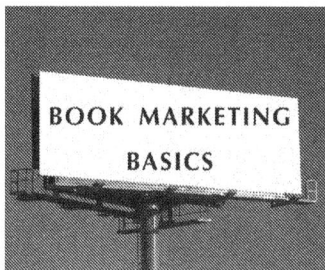

Another good way to promote your books is through the use of postcards or bookmarks. They are like the business cards of the book industry. These items are very inexpensive to produce, so you can use them liberally. You can print hundreds or thousands of them to hand out, mail, post on bulletin boards, etc. Let's face it, what author doesn't like to see his or her book cover on a postcard? And just as you have now included a caption at the end of all of your outgoing email, you should also include a bookmark or postcard in all of your outgoing regular mail. Even your regular payments and utility bills should include your bookmarks. After all, don't the banks and utility companies fill

their invoices with stuffers when they send them to you? It works: that's why they do it.

Before you hold a book signing, you should bring two or three hundred bookmarks or postcards and ask the venue's staff to hand them out before the event and also to include them in the bags of everyone purchasing books that day. If you simply make the effort to walk around the bookstore and hand out bookmarks or postcards yourself, you will see you sales double for the day.

It's also a good idea to have posters printed up to announce the event in advance. Aside from being easy, inexpensive advertising, it also lets the bookstore staff know you are a professional in the book industry. See **www.1stworldpublishing.com/printedmatter**

9. TALK RADIO

As it turns out, readers and book buyers also listen to talk radio. The simplest advice we can offer you is: purchase a copy of the Talk Radio Directory (it's relatively inexpensive) and contact every radio station on the list. You can acquire an updated list from: **www.xxxx** for a small amount of money.

> Talk radio sells more books than any other form of media.

Very Important: When you make your call to the talk show director, **be prepared**. Talk shows need to be interesting, exciting, informative, controversial, unique and beneficial, so you need to be enthusiastic about your book and its promotion. Producers of talk shows make their living by providing content to their listeners. If their guests are dull and unprofessional, it makes the talk show host look dull and unprofessional. So be prepared. Let the producer know you have a list of questions that his/her listeners would find intriguing and send him the list along with an information packet about your book. See **www.1stworldpublishing.com/talkshowquestions** for sample question sheets.

When you are ON THE AIR always be prepared to say: My book is available at: (_____).

You can always provide our 800 phone number or website address, but if you are doing a book signing or event in a specific location, you may want to send your listeners to that event or bookstore. You have to tell your listeners where you want them to buy your book. If all else fails, you can always say: available at bookstores everywhere.

10. WRITING PRESS RELEASES

Writing press releases has enormous value. If you have completed a full-length book, it is safe to say you like writing about the topic your book is about. To earn money from your book you must now learn to tell your story in a single page, and in a manner that makes the public stand in line to get a copy of your book. It is a fun and creative process; so don't cheat yourself out of the opportunity. Press releases are a free form of advertising, but without the stigma of a paid "buyer beware" ad. In many ways a press release is little more than glorified calendar listings. See **www.1stworldpublishing.com/PressReleases** for samples of effective press releases.

> To earn money from your book you must now learn to tell your story in a single page, and in a manner that makes the public stand in line to get a copy of your book.

Once your book is published and available in the market place, you should write many press releases. You should write a press release for every event or signing you do. You should write a press release every time a news agency runs a story that relates to the content of your book. As a service to our authors, we will distribute author-written press releases to approximately 300 national news agencies every month-or more, if the book is associated with an event or feature news article.

Next to talk radio, well-written press releases, when published, are one of the best ways to generate satisfactory book sales.

CHECKLIST

A. Press Releases
B. Book Reviewers
C. Key Newspapers

…and some great advice to help you get started

PART 3

SAMPLES & CONTACTS

A. SAMPLE PRESS RELEASES

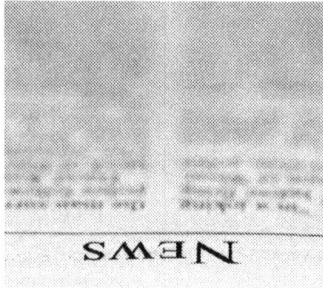

S W E N

The following are a few sample press releases to help you on your way to writing your own masterpiece.

Media Release
March 4, 2004
Contact: 1stWorld PR – 641-209-5000 . 877-209 5004

TIME TWISTS AND SHAPE SHIFTS
A Magical Caribbean Tale about the Mystery of the Soul

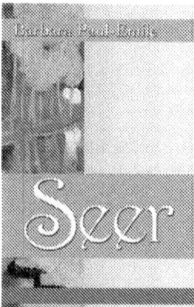

What if you could change time and re-chart your life? What different choices would you make?

Barbara Paul-Emile tackles these tantalizing questions in a magical tale of redemption set against the lush landscapes and spicy aromas of her native Jamaica. Her whirlwind magical mystery tour into other dimensions and alternate realities sweeps away the boundaries between the mystical and the mundane.

SEER tells the story of Becka, a wise shaman and psychic healer, and her spirited attempt to save the life of Jo-Jo, a young village boy in a near-death coma. To understand the nature of his sickness, Becka must journey in a trance to the deepest levels of Jo-Jo's soul. There she meets his fellow soul-travelers and the light-beings who guide them. Traveling through worlds of blinding light and shifting form, they contemplate the often terrible consequences of their actions on the earthly plane as they search for the ultimate understanding: We do not act in isolation. Our lives are part of a complex canvas of cause and effect.

Told in part in Jamaican patois and drawing on the rich mythic symbolism and animistic roots of her own Caribbean culture, Paul-Emile interweaves both poetry and song into her startling bright narrative about our existence outside the common framework of time and beyond the usual concept of normal.

Barbara Paul-Emile grew up in Jamaica where, in her words, "One could move freely between dimensions and contact ancestors and other spirits and energies to offer salutation or to ask for answers to troubling questions....people enjoyed a tapestry of life that was broader, more vibrant than commonly imagined". She is currently Professor of English and Maurice E. Goldman Distinguished Professor of Arts and Sciences at Bentley College, Waltham, MA, where her work centers on 19th century English Literature, Myth and Caribbean literature. She was named Massachusetts Professor of the Year for 1995. *SEER* is her first work of fiction.

SEER is available nationally in bookstores and through Internet retailers.

SEER, by Barbara Paul-Emile, Sunstar Publishing Ltd., March 2004

Soft Cover / ISBN: 1-887472-32-0 / 235 Pages / $17.95

Media Release
Sept. 10, 2006
Contact: 1stWorld PR – 641-209-5000 . 877-209 5004

Passion Test **Provides Hope for 120 Million Workers**

A 2005 study by Harris Interactive reported only 20% of American workers are passionate about what they do. With 151 million people in the workforce, that means over 120 million lack passion. A new book by Janet and Chris Attwood, "The Passion Test - The Effortless Path to Discovering Your Passion" offers hope for those who lack passion.

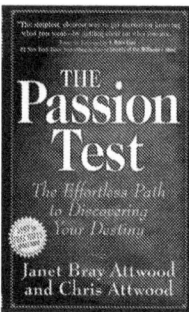

(PRWEB) September 6, 2006 - Today The Passion Test - The Effortless Path to Discovering Your Destiny went to #1 on the BarnesandNoble.com bestseller list. With a message that "when you are clear, what you want will show up in your life, and only to the extent you're clear," *The Passion Test* promises a simple, effective way to get aligned with what's most important.

A 2005 study by Harris Interactive reported only 20% of American workers are passionate about what they do. With 151 million people in the workforce, that means over 120 million people lack passion for their work.

Yet, business books are filled with the importance of passion and the business benefits of passion including:

1.) Increased focus
2.) More innovation and creativity
3.) Deeper commitment to values-driven business
4.) Increased performance
5.) Excitement and energy for work
6.) A sense of urgency which propels peak performance
7.) Overcoming fear
8.) Less attrition and absenteeism
9.) Greater perseverance
10.)Contagious enthusiasm

With over 80% of the workforce lacking in passion, business clearly hasn't solved the passion puzzle.

This new book by Janet and Chris Attwood promises to unlock the key to the passion enigma.

Chicken Soup for the Soul author Jack Canfield took The Passion Test and reported:

"*The Passion Test* has given me incredible insight into what was missing in my life, where I was not 100% spot-on in pursuing my passions. It's simple, it's easy, and it's profound. Out of it came the creation of an organization I'd been putting off for six years and a fuller expression of my love and my commitment to my family"

Perhaps *The Passion Test* is the secret business needs to motivate those 120 million Americans who lack passion.

FOR IMMEDIATE RELEASE

1st World Publishing
contact: Mira Waller
Director of Marketing
641-209-5000
mira@1stworldpublishing.com
Date: March, 27th 2007

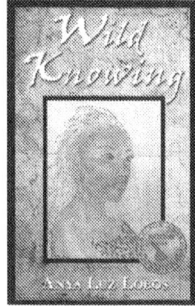

Just Published!

A New Voice in Visionary Fiction

Wild Knowing is delicious, moving and beautiful. With a bracing simplicity of language it takes us to a distant world, then pulls away our internal moorings, leaving us to question our most basic assumptions. Author Anya Luz Lobos, winner of the Chelson Award in fiction, has an inimitable voice, feminine and brilliantly evocative.

A story of profound romantic/erotic love, *Wild Knowing* follows one man's unique journey to enlightenment. It delves into the inner realms of archetype and primal desire, and opens up new dimensions of spirituality and consciousness for the reader. Memorably expressed, without laboring the point, *Wild Knowing* provides an almost visceral sense of higher states of consciousness, but not before exposing the fears that prevent such realization. *Wild Knowing* has a heart-stopping plot: the author weaves wisdom through darkness as well as light.

Diane Frank, author of *Blackberries in the Dream House* described *Wild Knowing* as "a higher love story with an impeccable sense of ethics-an interplanetary page turner with large ideas, written in the voice of the Wise Woman."

John Daniel, author of *The Poet's Funeral* writes, "Set on the planet Daria, *Wild Knowing* pairs a man from Earth with a wise and beautiful Darian woman. What the man learns about love from this absorbing experience would benefit us all."

Author Rodney Charles (*Every Day a Miracle Happens*) describes *Wild Knowing* as "a healing balm. It is an extraordinary odyssey told with the sensitive passion of a woman's wisdom. Beautifully written, with eloquent assurance, the author weaves a story that invites us to explore the very real world of intuitive love."

Anya Luz Lobos is also the author of the novel Seaspring. Raised in both Nicaragua and the United States, she is a performance artist who combines dramatic interpretation of literature with Expressive Sign Language.

Books will be available through bookstores everywhere starting May 4th, 2007.

Spanish Translation to be released summer 2007

Title: Wild Knowing
Author: Anya Luz Lobos
ISBN: 1-59540-832-0
Publisher: 1st World Publishing
www.1stworldpublishing.com
Page Count: 304
Retail Price: $18.95
Date of Release: May 4th, 2007

Media Release
May 10, 2007
Contact: 1stWorld PR – 641-209-5000 . 877-209 5004

Little Boy, Big Book

I keep hearing that children are growing up quicker these days, but I didn't know they were making career choices at the age of eight. My son is a normal boy-he loves sports, bugs, Pokeman, dinosaurs and planets-but ever since he appropriated my laptop, he's discovered that all knowledge is available via the internet. Google has the answer to all of his questions: What to feed his pet turtle? What planets have we landed on? What Pokeman is rarest? He has also discovered that he can organize his new knowledge and create books with the use of his (my) computer.

One year ago, he wrote a story (typing with two fingers) about how his father had inadvertently swallowed a scientific potion and shrunk himself smaller than an ant. Fortunately for the child, this occurred on show-and-tell day at school. Thus, the title: DAD AND ME GO TO SCHOOL.

I won't spoil the ending for you, but needless to say, when my wife and I first read this masterpiece, we were bursting with pride. I quickly taught him how to download copyright-free illustrations from the internet, and before long he surpassed my internet skills and organized a wonderful children's book of his own.

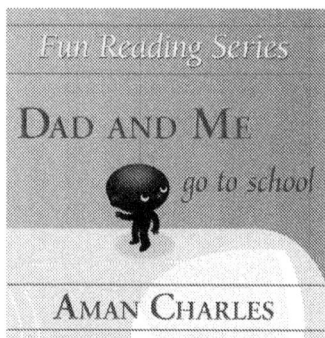

Fun Reading Series

DAD AND ME
go to school

AMAN CHARLES

As a writer and publisher, I knew I could easily publish his book through my own company (1stWorld Publishing... no plug intended). He agreed, and we did it.

His book has now been published for 4 months and he is organizing readings, signings, talks with reading groups, presentations at schools, email campaigns, etc. He has hired his 13-year-old sister, Anya, to be his editor-manager-agent, and his June-July royalty check promises to be bigger than my own. Go figure.

B. BOOK REVIEW EDITORS

I always recommend that authors send out as many **eGalleys** as they can, as long as they are intelligently targeted (not Spam). However, the Top 12 Book Reviewers listed below are an elite group and will surely produce many sales of your book should they chose to review it. For that reason, it is wise to send Hard Copy Galleys of your book to these 12 reviewers. Be sure to send your galleys 3 to 4 months before your release date. If you don't, the reviewers won't bother to look at them.

You probably won't need phone numbers, and as a general rule, editors and their phone numbers change every 10 months. These days, phone numbers are easily available online, but it's a good idea to check with the editor in question first if you feel the need to make phone contact.

When you send your eGalley or Hard Copy Galley through the mail, be sure to include a cover letter (keep it brief—one page maximum) and a list of any reviews or endorsements you may have already collected. Following are samples of both a **Cover Letter** and an **Endorsement List. These** documents will assist you in easily creating your own marketing materials.

Top 12 Book Reviewers

1. Publishers Weekly
2. Kirkus Reviews
3. Booklist, American Library Association
4. Library Journal
5. New York Times Book Review
6. USA Today
7. Washington Post
8. Bloomsbury Review
9. New York Review of Books
10. Chicago Tribune
11. Los Angeles Times
12. San Francisco Chronicle

Publishers Weekly, 360 Park Avenue South, 13th Floor, New York NY
10010-1710; 646-746-6400; Fax: 646-746-6631.
Web: http://www.publishersweekly.com.

Kirkus Reviews, 770 Broadway, New York, NY 10003-9595; 646-654-4602 or
646-654-5500; Fax: 646-654-4706.
Email: kirkusrev@kirkusreviews.com.
Web: http://www.kirkusreviews.com.

Booklist, American Library Association, 50 E. Huron Street, Chicago, IL 60611-2729; 312-944-6780; 800-545-2433; Fax: 312-337-6787.
Email: bsmothers@ala.org.
Web: http://www.ala.org.

Library Journal, 360 Park Avenue South, 13th Floor, New York NY 10010-1710; 646-746-6400; Fax: 646-746-6734.
Email: lj@reedbusiness.com
or ljquery@reedbusiness.com.
Web: http://www.libraryjournal.com.
Submission guidelines at
http://www.ljdigital.com/about/submission.asp.

New York Times Book Review, 229 West 43rd Street, New York, NY 10036;
212-556-1234; Fax: 212-556-3690. Book review phone: 212-556-7366.
Web: http://www.nytimes.com/books.
Charles McGrath is editor of the Book Review.
Eden Lipson is children's book editor.
Christopher Lehmann-Haupt (212-556-4885), Michiko Kakutani (212-556-4874), and Richard Bernstein (212-556-4050) are the chief book critics for the daily New York Times.

USA Today, 7950 Jones Branch Drive, McLean VA 22108; 703-854-3400;
800-USA-0001; Fax: 703-854-2053.
Web: http://www.usatoday.com.

Washington Post Book World, 1150 15th Street N.W., Washington, DC 20071;
202-334-6000; Fax: 202-334-7502.
Web: http://www.washingtonpost.com.
Marie Arana, Editor. Jonathan Yardley, Book Critic (202-334-7883).

The Bloomsbury Review, Owaissa Communications, 1553 Platte Street #206,
Denver, CO 80202-1167; 303-455-3123;
Fax: 303-455-7039.
Email: bloomsb@aol.com.
Tom Auer, Editor-in-Chief.

New York Review of Books, 1755 Broadway, 5th Floor, New York, NY
10019-3780; 212-757-8070; Fax: 212-333-5374.
Email: mail@nybooks.com.
Web: http://www.nybooks.com.
Robert B. Silvers and Barbara Epstein, Editors.

Chicago Tribune, Attn: Books, 435 N. Michigan Avenue #400, Chicago IL 60611-4022; 312-222-3232; Fax: 312-222-3143 or 312-222-0236 (features).
Web: http://www.chicagotribune.com.
Elizabeth Taylor, Literary Editor.
Email: etaylor@tribune.com.
Mary Harris Russell, Book Reviewer, Children's Corner.

Los Angeles Times Book Review, 202 West 1st Street, Los Angeles CA 90012; 213-237-7001; Fax: 213-237-4712.
Web: http://www.latimes.com.
Editorial staff: http://www.latimes.com/services/newspaper/mediacenter/la-mediacenter-editorial-staff,0,1090476.story.

San Francisco Chronicle, 901 Mission Street, San Francisco, CA 94103; 415-777-6258; Fax: 415-957-8737.
Email: bookrev@sfchronicle.com.
Web: http://www.sfgate.com.
Oscar Villalon, Book Review Editor.
Email: ovillalon@sfchronicle.com.
Reagan McMahon reviews books.
Email: mcmahon@sfchronicle.com.

Book: The Magazine for the Reading Life,
Jerome Kramer, Editor, West Egg Communications, 252 West 37th Street, 5th Floor, New York, NY 10018; 212-659-7070; Fax: 212-736-4455.
Email: jkramer@bookmagazine.com.
Web: http://www.bookmagazine.com.
Elaine Szewczyk, Book Review Editor.

Book Street USA, BethFhaner, Editor, Creation Integrated Media, 5880 Oberlin Drive, San Diego, CA 92121; 858-812-6488; Fax: 858-450-3555.
Email: editor@bookstreetusa.com.
Web: http://www.bookstreetusa.com.
A full-color, monthly book review reaching 2 million homes.

Boston Book Review, 331 Harvard Street #17, Cambridge, MA 02139; 617-497-0344; Fax: 617-497-0394. Email: BBR-Info@BostonBookReview.com. Web: http://www.BostonBookReview.com. Theoharis Constantine Theoharis, Editor. Kiril Stefan Alexandrov, Book Editor.

ForeWord, 129½ E. Front Street, Traverse City, MI 49684; 231-933-3699; Fax: 231-933-3899. Email: reviews@traverse.com. Web: http://www.forewordmagazine.com. Alex Moore, Managing Review Editor.

Voice Literary Supplement, Village Voice, 36 Cooper Square, New York, NY 10003-4846; 212-475-3300; Fax: 212-475-8944. Email: jpress@villagevoice.com. Web: http://www.villagevoice.com/vls. Joy Press, Literary Editor.

Rain Taxi Review of Books, Eric Lorberer, Editor, P O Box 3840, Minneapolis, MN 55403. Email: raintaxi@bitstream.net. Web: http://www.raintaxi.com. A quarterly review for poetry and nonfiction books.

Ruminator Review, 1648 Grand Avenue,
St. Paul, MN 55105; 651-699-2610;
Fax: 651-699-7190.
Email: review@ruminator.com.
Web: http://www.ruminator.com.
Margaret Todd Maitland, Editor. Eleise Jones,
Children's Books.
Published quarterly and distributed through inde-
pendent bookstores around the country.

Romantic Times, 55 Bergen Street, Brooklyn, NY
11201; 718-237-1097; Fax:
718-624-4231.
Email: kfalk@romantictimes.com.
Web: http://www.romantictimes.com.
Kathryn Falk, Publisher.

(Sample <u>Cover Letter</u> for Book Reviews)

Date

Name (Reviewer)
Company
Address
City/State/Zip
Email

Dear   ,

> Title: Alice Hoax
> Author: (Name)
> ISBN: 123-4-567-8901-23
> Category:Historic Fiction /Literary Fiction
> Size: 5.5 x 8.5
> Page Count: 650 pages
> Price: 25.95 Cloth Cover
> Release Date: (allow 3-4 months advance
> notice)

Please find enclosed an advanced copy of ALICE HOAX for your review.

We are at a loss for words as to where to begin with this work. It is a masterpiece and must be published. This is not a dry work of scholarship. The author is compelled to reveal the truths of the Alice Books and does so in a manner that will satisfy almost every palette, from that of the serious scholar to that of the curious layman. There is never a moment in the entire 600+ pages that the writing does not feel inspired.

The author posses an enormous background in research on Queen Victoria (and Lewis Carroll) and the novel is so cleverly intertwined with both scholarly fact and a superbly crafted fictional storyline, more intuitive than inventive, that it is near impossible not to believe that Tenniel himself (Alice's Illustrator) did not write it.

You will find yourself revisiting your childhood, re-exposed to the Alice images, but this time through the eyes of angels (or Tenneil) who knew the "hoax" in the making. St. Cloud lays down a multi-flavored, factual scenario that is spiced with intrigue, betrayal, conspiracy and secrecy. Not only will you be subsumed with the biographies and autobiographies of Queen Victoria, Louis

Napoleon, John Tenneil, Prince Albert and Charles Dodgson, but you will also revel in the author's mastery of Victorian English, which is equally rich with content, not to mention the personal warmth, wisdom and Shakespearian flare of the author's own creative voice.

Note: Try to unravel the obvious mystery in the author's pseudonym. Alas, your powers of perception may fall short. You may find there is something in the miracles accredited to St. Cloud and the removal of the clouds of illusion ...

This book has been guided very carefully every step of the way, from editing, formatting and cover design to marketing (see marketing plan and endorsement sheet enclosed).

If you have any questions, don't hesitate to contact us.

Sincerely,

Rodney Charles
Editor
rodney@1stworldlibrary.org

(Sample Endorsement Sheet for Book Reviewers)

Reviews and Endorsements

"With poetic language that gracefully reveals the vibrant, lush world of Kyoto to the reader, Frank gracefully tells the story of two lovers eternally bound by fate and time."
—*Booklist*: Kristine Huntley, Reviewer

"*Blackberries in the Dream House* is an elegiac and erotic tale about the forbidden love between a geisha and a Buddhist monk named Kenji in Kyoto, Japan a century and a half ago......*Blackberries* concerns the deepest meaning of love. Filled with the sensual delights of two bodies in love, this novel flows with color and texture."
—*Santa Cruz Sentinel*: Chris Watson, Book Editor

"What would happen to us if we were to undertake the discipline of turning our life entirely and self-consciously, into a poem? Through Yukiko, who becomes both a contemplative Buddhist and a geisha skilled in the refinements of sensuous pleasure, Diane Frank allows us to live within the soul of a young woman who has undertaken to create a life imagined and expressed as a poem, in every moment, waking and sleeping, making love or meditating. With its power of language, *Blackberries in the Dream House* will seduce many readers into considering whether a prosaic life is the only choice we have."
—Pierre DeLattre
Author of *Walking on Air* and *Tales of a Dalai Lama*

"Diane Frank's exquisite sensibility manifests throughout in Blackberries in the Dream House; it is both erotic and metaphysical. In fact, her great strength is that for her there's no division between the two. The result is this fine lyrical novel."
—Stephen Dunn
Pulitzer Prize-winning poet

"*Blackberries in the Dream House* is written in beautiful prose, like linear poetry. This novel is carefully crafted, full of exotic images, very soft, no hard edges, just beautiful."

—Nick Lawrence
NPR Affiliate, WUKY-FM, *Curtains at Eight!*

"*Blackberries in the Dream House* gets to you like a caress from the most longed-for and tender of lovers. It turns you on and heals your heart. Diane Frank is a poet goddess whose exquisite incantation will leave you naked in your own sacred house of dreams."

—Alan James Mayer
Talk Show Host, Radio Producer

"*Blackberries in the Dream House* made me weep from its beauty. The language is breathtaking, the story is delicious, and the book is filled with light."

—Jennifer Hawthorne, Bestselling Author
Chicken Soup for the Woman's Soul

Diane Frank's story is a metaphysical romance novel written in delicately poetic prose. When her heroin, Yukiko, is happy, butterflies fill her hair and hummingbirds fly out of her mouth. The lovers don't make physical love so much as meld into one being.

—*Des Moines Register*,
Ellen Heath, Book Editor

"*Blackberries in the Dream House* reads like an altered state of consciousness. Its powerful language and exotic love story combine to create a deep impression that lasts far beyond the end of the book."

—John Kremer, Author
1001 Ways to Market Your Books

"Reading *Blackberries in the Dream House* is like reading one continuous prose poem. You step into a floating world of piercing beauty, wild magic, and earth-shaking emotions. For days I walked around dazed, lost in the dream."

—Caree Connet
Award-winning poet

"The novel meets the poem in this lovely book with the most exquisite seamlessness. The beauty of language and image Diane Frank is able to maintain, line after line, seems to flirt with the miraculous."

—Nancy Berg
Award-winning poet

"When you remove everything that is not necessary, something glows underneath. This novel glows with Diane Frank's poetic and visionary wisdom, through an erotic journey illuminating universal cycles of birth, death and rebirth. After having immersed yourself in the sacred lives of Yukiko, a geisha, and the young monk, Kenji, in an older, artistically flowering Japan, you might feel, as I did, along with Yukiko, 'My feet are slices of melon, birds curling over rocks. Where have they taken me now?'"

—Diane Averill
Author of *Beautiful Obstacles*

"*Blackberries in the Dream House* is a passionate novel written by a poet. It is told using deeply saturated images by a woman who lives with vibrating intensity. Frank has a keen eye for the terror and majesty of falling in love, and a kind heart for the circuitous paths the heart takes to escape."

—Terry Brennan
Reviewer, *The Chicago Reader*

(Sample <u>Cover Letter</u> for Book Reviews)

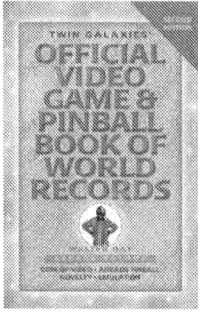

Title: Twin Galaxies - Book of World Records
Author: Walter Day
ISBN: 123-4-567-8901-23
Category: Reference
Size: 6 x 9
Page Count: 850 pages
Price: 24.95 (Perfect Bound)
Release Date: June 1, 2007

Edited by Twin Galaxies' Chief Scorekeeper, Walter Day, and Senior Editor Mr. Kelly R. Flewin, *Twin Galaxies' Official Video Game & Pinball Book of World Records* honors arcade champions from the last thirty years and celebrates the greatest achievements in Arcade Video Games, Arcade Emulation, Novelty Games and Arcade Pinball.

Walter Day, the historical founder of organized video game playing, and the Twin Galaxies Intergalactic Scoreboard continues to verify world record scores on all gaming platforms—from the classic Atari 2600 home system of yesteryear to today's modern Xbox Live and Playstation 3.

Twin Galaxies' Intergalactic Scoreboard maintains an online presence at www.twingalaxies.com, where gamers can obtain updated information on all world record scores and game-playing rules.

Marketing

- $30,000 marketing budget
- Four-state author tour: Florida, California, Kansas, Colorado
- National press release campaign
- National radio tour
- National and international viral email campaigns
- National and regional print publicity
- Consumer and trade advertising
- Regional seminars and lectures (Iowa and Illinois)

C. KEY NEWSPAPERS THAT REVIEW BOOKS

Below are additional newspaper contacts that you may find useful:

Albuquerque Journal, Books Editor, 7777 Jefferson NE (87109-4343), P.O. Drawer J, Albuquerque NM 87103; 505-823-4400. Web: http://www.abqjournal.com.

Anchorage Daily News, Books Editor, 1001 Northway Drive (99508-2098), P O Box 149001, Anchorage AK 99514-9001; 907-257-4200. Web: http://www.adn.com.

The Arizona Republic, Books Editor, 200 E Van Buren, Phoenix AZ 85004; 602-444-8432; Fax: 602-444-2417. Web: http://www.arizonarepublic.com

Atlanta Journal-Constitution, Books Editor, 72 Marietta Street, Atlanta GA 30303; 404-526-5377; Fax: 404-526-5766. Web: http://www.ajc.com.

Austin American Statesman, Books Editor, 305 S. Congress Avenue (78704), P.O. Box 670, Austin, TX 78767; 512-445-3720; Fax: 512-445-3968. Web: http://www.Austin360.com

Baltimore Sun, Books Editor, 501 N Calvert Street (21202); P O Box 1377, Baltimore MD 21278. 410-332-6000; 800-829-8000, ext. 6223. Web: http://www.baltimoresun.com.

The Baton Rouge Advocate, Books Editor, P O Box 558, Baton Rouge, LA 70821-0588; 225-383-1111. Web: http://www.2theadvocate.com.

Boston Globe, Books Editor, 135 Morrissey Boulevard, P.O. Box 2378, Boston, MA 02107; 617-929-2000. Web: http://www.boston.com.

Boston Herald, Book Editor, 1 Herald Square, P.O. Box 55843, Boston MA 02205; 617-426-3000; Fax: 617-451-3506. Arts & Lifestyle: 617-619-6193. Web: http://www.bostonherald.com.

Buffalo News, Books Editor, Gusto, One News Plaza, P.O. Box 100, Buffalo, NY 14240; 800-777-8680; Fax: 716-856-5150. Web: http://www.buffalonews.com.

Charlotte Observer, Books Editor, 600 S. Tryon Street, Charlotte NC 28202; 704-358-5234; Fax: 704-358-5036. Web: http://www.charlotteobserver.com.

Chicago Sun-Times, Books Editor, 350 N. Orleans Street, 10th Floor, Chicago IL 60654; 312-321-3000. Web: http://www.suntimes.com. One of the ten largest newspapers in the U.S. "Each week we offer free local listings of author readings and feature an interview with a local author."

Chicago Tribune, Attn: Books, 435 N. Michigan Avenue #400, Chicago IL 60611-4022; 312-222-3232; Fax: 312-222-3143. Web: http://www.chicagotribune.com. Elizabeth Taylor, Literary Editor. Email: etaylor@tribune.com.

Christian Science Monitor, Books Editor, One Norway Street, Boston, MA 02115; 617-450-2000; Fax: 617-450-7575. Web: http://www.csmonitor.com.

Cincinnati Enquirer, Books Editor, 312 Elm Street, Library, 19th Floor, Cincinnati OH 45202; 513-768-8380; Fax: 513-768-8330. Web: http://news.enquirer.com.

Cleveland Plain Dealer, Books Editor, 1801 Superior Avenue NE, Cleveland, OH 44114-2107; 216-999-5000; Fax: 216-999-6354.

Dallas Morning News, Books Editor, 508 Young Street, Dallas TX 75202; 214-977-8408. Web: http://www.dallasnews.com.

The Denver Post, Books Editor, 1560 Broadway, Denver CO 80202-1577; P.O. Box 1709 Denver C 80201; 303-820-1624; 800-336-7678; Fax: 303-820-1679. Web: http://www.denverpost.com. Editors: http://www.denverpost.com/contactus.

Detroit Free Press, Books Editor, 321 W Lafayette Boulevard, Detroit MI 48231; 313-223-4530; Fax: 313-223-4726. Web: http://www.freep.com.

South Florida Sun-Sentinel, Books Editor, 200 E. Las Olas Boulevard, Fort Lauderdale, FL 33301-2293; 954-356-4710; Fax: 954-356-4612. Web: http://www.sun-sentinel.com.

Fort Worth Star-Telegram, Books Editor, 400 West 7th Street (76102), P O Box 1870, Fort Worth TX 76115; 817-390-7720. Web: http://www.dfw.com/mld/dfw.

Hartford Courant, Books Editor, 285 Broad Street, Hartford CT 06115; 860-241-6200; Web: http://www.courant.com.

The Honolulu Advertiser, Books Editor, 605 Kapiolani Boulevard (96813), P.O. Box 3110, Honolulu HI 96802; 808-535-2412; Fax: 808-525-8055. Web: http://www.honoluluadvertiser.com.

Houston Chronicle, Books Editor, 801 Texas Avenue (77002), P.O. Box 4260, Houston, TX 77210; 713-362-7171. Web: http://www.chron.com.

Indianapolis Star, Books Editor, 307 N. Pennsylvania Street, Indianapolis IN 46204; 317-444-4000. Web: http://www.indystar.com.

International Herald Tribune, Books Editor, 6 bis, rue des Graviers, 92521 Neuilly Cedex, France; (33-1) 41 43 93 22; Fax: (33-1) 41 43 93 32. General email: iht@iht.com. Web: http://www.iht.com.

Kansas City Star, Books Editor, 1729 Grand Boulevard, Kansas City MO 64108-1413; 816-234-4141; Fax: 816-234-4926. Web: http://www.kcstar.com.

Los Angeles Times Book Review, 202 West 1st Street, Los Angeles CA 90012; 213-237-7001; Fax: 213-237-4712. Web: http://www.latimes.com.

Louisville Courier-Journal, Books Editor, 525 W Broadway, P O Box 740031, Louisville KY 40201-7431; 502-582-4011; Fax: 502-582-4066. Web: http://www.courier-journal.com.

Miami Herald, Books Editor, One Herald Plaza, Miami, FL 33132-1693; 305-376-3649; Fax: 305-376-8950. Web: http://www.herald.com.

Milwaukee Journal Sentinel, Books Editor, 333 W. State Street, P.O. Box 371, Milwaukee, WI 53201; 414-224-2000. Web: http://www.jsonline.com.

Minneapolis Star Tribune, Books Editor, 425 Portland Avenue South, Minneapolis, MN 55488; 612-673-4380; Fax: 612-673-7568. Web: http://www.startribune.com.

New Orleans Times-Picayune, Books Editor, 3800 Howard Avenue, New Orleans, LA 70125-1429; 504-826-3457; 800-925-0000; Fax: 504-826-3186. Web: http://www.timespicayune.com.

New York Daily News, Books Editor, 450 West 33rd Street, New York, NY 10001; 212-210-2100; Fax: 212-643-7831. Web: http://www.nydailynews.com.

New York Observer, Books Editor, 915 Broadway, 9th Floor, New York, NY 10010; 212-755-2400; Fax: 212-688-4889. Web: http://www.observer.com.

New York Post, Books Editor, 1211 Avenue of the Americas, New York, NY 10036; 212-930-8000; Fax: 212-930-8542. Web: http://www.nypost.com.

New York Times Books Editor, 229 West 43rd Street, New York, NY 10036; 212-556-1234; Fax: 212-556-3690. Web: http://www.nytimes.com/books.

Newark Star-Ledger, Books Editor, 1 Star-Ledger Plaza, Newark, NJ 07102; 973-392-4040. Web: http://www.starledger.com.

Newsday, Books Editor, 235 Pinelawn Road, Melville NY 11747-4250. Web: http://www.newsday.com. Arts & Entertainment Editor, 2 Park Avenue, 8th Floor, New York NY 10016-5695; 212-251-6622.

Orlando Sentinel, Books Editor, 633 N. Orange Avenue, Orlando FL 32801; 407-420-5135; Web: http://www.orlandosentinel.com.

Philadelphia Inquirer, Books Editor, 400 N. Broad Street, Philadelphia PA 19130; 215-854-5615; Fax: 215-854-5099. Web: http://www.philly.com.

Pittsburgh Post-Gazette, Books Editor, 34 Boulevard of the Allies (15222), P O Box 566, Pittsburgh PA 15230; 412-263-1601; Fax: 412-391-8452. Web: http://www.post-gazette.com.

Pittsburgh Tribune-Review, Books Editor, Building, 503 Martindale Street, 3rd Floor, Pittsburgh PA 15212 ; 412-320-7990. Web: http://www.pittsburghlive.com.

Portland Oregonian, Books Editor, 1320 S.W. Broadway, Portland OR 97201-9911; 503-221-8150; 877-238-8221; Fax: 503-294-4193. Web: http://www.oregonlive.com.

Providence Journal-Bulletin, Books Editor, 75 Fountain Street, Providence RI 02902; 401-277-7000; Fax: 401-277-7346. Web: http://www.projo.com.

Rocky Mountain News, Books Editor, 400 W Colfax Avenue, Denver CO 80204; 303-892-5000; Fax: 303-892-5001. Web: http://www.RockyMountainNews.com.

Sacramento Bee, Books Editor, 2100 Q Street, P O Box 15779, Sacramento CA 95852; 916-321-1000; Fax: 916-321-1109. Saint Louis Post-Dispatch, Book Review Editor, 900 N. Tucker Boulevard, Saint Louis, MO 63101; 314-340-8107; Fax: 314-340-3080. Web: http://www.stltoday.com. Main phone: 314-340-8000.

Saint Petersburg Times, Books Editor, 490 First Avenue S (33701), P.O. Box 1121, Saint Petersburg FL 33731; 727-893-8435; 800-333-7505. Web: http://www.sptimes.com.

San Antonio Express-News, Books Editor, Avenue E & 3rd Street (78205), P O Box 2171, San Antonio TX 78297-2171; 210-225-7411; Fax: 210-229-9268.

San Diego Union-Tribune, Books Editor, P.O. Box 120191, San Diego, CA 92112-0191; 619-293-1321; 800-244-6397; Fax: 619-293-2436. Web: http://www.uniontrib.com.

San Francisco Chronicle, 901 Mission Street, San Francisco, CA 94103; 415-777-6258; Fax: 415-957-8737. Web: http://www.sfgate.com.

Santa Fe New Mexican, Books Editor, 202 E Marcy Street (87501), P O Box 2048, Santa Fe NM 87504-2048; 505-995-3878. Web: http://www.santafenewmexican.com.

Seattle Post-Intelligencer, Book Review Editor, 101 Elliot Avenue West, Seattle WA 98119-4220; 206-448-8170; Fax: 206-448-8166. Web: http://www.seattlepi.com.

Seattle Times, Books Editor, 1120 John Street, Seattle WA 98109; 206-464-2357. Web: http://www.seattletimes.com

Tampa Tribune, Books Editor, The News Center, 200 S. Parker Street (33606-2395), P.O. Box 191, Tampa, FL 33601-0191; 813-259-7711; 813-259-7600. Web: http://www.tampatrib.com.

Toronto Star, Books Editor and Literary Critic. Web: http://www.thestar.com.

Tucson Citizen and Arizona Daily Star, Books Editor, 4850 S. Park Avenue, P O Box 26887, Tucson AZ 85726; 520-573-4511; Fax: 520-573-4109. Web: http://www.azstarnet.com and http://www.tucsoncitizen.com.

USA Today, Books Editor, 7950 Jones Branch Drive, McLean VA 22108; 703-854-3400; 800-USA-0001; Fax: 703-854-2053. Web: http://www.usatoday.com.

Voice Literary Supplement, Books Editor, Village Voice, 36 Cooper Square, New York NY 10003-4846; 212-475-3300; Fax: 212-475-8944. Web: http://www.villagevoice.com/vls.

Wall Street Journal, Books Editor, Dow Jones & Company, 200 Liberty Street, New York, NY 10281; 212-416-2000. Web: http://www.wsj.com.

Washington Post Book World, Books Editor, 1150 15th Street
N.W., Washington, DC 20071; 202-334-6000;
Fax: 202-334-7502.
Web: http://www.washingtonpost.com.
Book World web: http://www.washingtonpost.com/wp-dyn/content/print/bookworld/index.html.

Washington Times, Books Editor, 3600 New York Avenue NE,
Washington DC 20002-1947; Main phone: 202-636-3000.
Fax: 202-832-2235. Web: http://www.washingtontimes.com.

Westchester Journal-News, Books Editor, One Gannett Drive,
White Plains NY 10604; 914-694-9300;
Fax: 914-696-8396.
Web: http://www.thejournalnews.com.

About the Author

Rodney Charles is an innovative, self-motivated entrepreneur and business leader who conceived the 1stWorld Publishing business while acting as President and Managing Editor of his own self-built book publishing company, Sunstar Publishing Ltd. (1992). His diverse experiences, ranging from media management, business-to-business aggregation and hands-on daily interaction with authors and publishers, have resulted in the assembly of many of the resources required to implement 1st World. He has authored six books: *The Land of Love, Art & Genius; Lighter Than Air; The Name Book*; (editor) *Publish It Now* and the best-selling *Every Day a Miracle Happens*.

Notes

1st World Publishing

1100 North 4th Street
Gate Ridge Court Bldg.
Fairfield, IA 52556
tel: 641/209-5000
Email: **info@1stworldpublishing.com**
Web: **www.1stworldpublishing.com**

Notes

Notes

Notes

Notes

Notes

Notes

Notes

Notes

Notes

Notes

Notes

Notes

Notes

Notes

Notes

Notes

Notes

Notes

Notes

Notes

Notes

Notes